Matt Stadd Embraces Life

Matt Stadd Embraces Life

An anthology

© Matt Stadd, 2024

Published by Diamond Geezer Publishing

All rights reserved. No part of this book may be reproduced, adapted, stored in a retrieval system or transmitted by any means, electronic, mechanical, photocopying, or otherwise without the prior written permission of the author.

The rights of Matt Stadd to be identified as the author of this work have been asserted in accordance with the Copyright, Designs and Patents Act 1988.

A CIP catalogue record for this book is available from the British Library.

ISBN 978-1-5262-0997-9

Cover design by Gabriela Berardi

Prepared and printed by:

York Publishing Services Ltd
64 Hallfield Road
Layerthorpe
York YO31 7ZQ

Tel: 01904 431213

Website: www.yps-publishing.co.uk

For My Darling Linda

CONTENTS

About the author	1
Foreword	3
Quotation : Oscar Wilde	6
The Truth	7
Loss of Freedom	8
Thoughts of a Young Soul	9
A New Relationship	11
The Ward at Night	12
The Nurse	13
Matthew	14
"We Will Rock You"	15
Quotation : P.G. Wodehouse	18
Diamond Geezer	19
A Day in the Bay	22
Bound for Aviemore	25
Paul and Dierdre and Carol and Me	28
Duncan, Graeme, Sam – Tweed	30
Skylark	32
Quotation : W.H. Auden	34
Stick with Me, Honey	35
The Pig 'n Pastry	38

Rhyming Antonyms	40
If Shakespeare was Sonnet, can I have some, please!!	43
On a Spanish Strand	44
Marathon Girls	45
Link in My Chain	47
Cup Final Day	49
Rave on at the Clarendon	54
Something Great!!!	56
Imaginative Play	59
World Cup 2022	64
Similes : Ancient and Modern	68
Anxiety	73
Be Thankful for the Music	75
Limerick : anonymous	77
Appropriately Named	78
I Have a New Pal	82
The Garden Room	86
Wonderful Afternoon in Busot	87
The Pasta Menu	89
Golden Oldies	91
Party Invitation	98
Culham Reunion 2023	100
Just My Cuppa	103
Orkney Trip	104
Do Not Touch It!!	109
For Frances and Paul	110

ABOUT THE AUTHOR

MATT STADD, aka ALAN HORNE, attended West St Leonards Primary, Hastings Grammar and Culham College. He has a Bachelor of Education Honours degree and taught in South East London for very nearly forty years.

He has variously been a paper-boy, pot-boy, bank clerk, rating officer, assistant bailiff, deck chair attendant, bus conductor, telephone salesman, postman, footballer, cricketer, golfer, lawn-bowler, hill-walker, dale-walker, dog-walker, volunteer, traveller, hitch-hiker, race-goer, art-lover, and writer of poetry.

During a prolonged period in hospital with a fractured leg, he began to put thoughts to paper, and wrote his first poem in August 1971.

Today the poetry force is with him more than ever.

Alan is now retired and living in York.

FOREWORD

Far too many of us are suspicious of poetry, tending to be a little afraid of things we do not understand.

"Poetry and poets are soft."

"Poetry won't help you to get on in life."

"Poetry may be all very well for arty types, but it's no use to the man in the street."

The men-in-the-street in ancient Greece flocked in crowds to watch poetic drama.

Medieval minstrels and ballad singers were hugely popular in towns and villages with their recitals of poetry.

The Elizabethan man-in-the-street loved the poetic works of Shakespeare.

For me, poetry brightens up words that once looked ordinary. It may coin new words, put words into a new context, enriching the value of written language.

Poetry, through the use of words, is an art form which tells us about the world through our feelings. It can sharpen our senses, exercise our imagination, and store treasure in our memory.

My poetry is mostly characterised by metre and rhyme. Rhymes generally come at the end of lines; the ear learns to expect a rhyme, and is pleased when it's there.

I hope that my poems are easy to read, and to understand. I want them to be universally accessible.

Many of my poems are drawn from personal experience.

I hope that some will make you stop and think, and that some will make you smile.

Note: Excessive rhyme may seriously impair your health.
Consume responsibly.

In promulgating your esoteric cogitations, or articulating your superficial sentimentalities and amicable philosophical or psychological observations, beware of platitudinous ponderosity.

Let your conversational communications possess a clarified conciseness, a compacted comprehensibleness, coalescent consistency, and a concatenated cogency.

Shun prurient jocosity and pestiferous profanity, obscurant or apparent.

Anonymous.

"All poetry, good or bad, springs from genuine feeling."

Oscar Wilde

THE TRUTH

I tell not a lie
I tell not one fib
I've broken one fib
I've broken one tib …
The x-ray proved it.

August 1971

LOSS OF FREEDOM

Yesterday I was my own master,
to run at will.
If only I could have run just
    that bit faster
I might have avoided this
    minor disaster.
But now, alas, I have
    a new master,
a three foot long plaster.
And I'll not run at will …
    Until?

August 1971

THOUGHTS OF A YOUNG SOUL

I wish I could go home.
Home says 'Welcome', and you
    know you are safe.
This room is like a cell.
At times the confines of the cell
    begin to close in all around,
requiring intense mental effort
    to repel them.

Everyone is very kind and
    I am well looked after.
But nothing compares to the
    attentions of your loved one.
Soon I shall be at home, with
    my brow on my wife's breast,
    and my mind will ache less.
The pain of the mind is more
    intense than that of the body,
as I lay entombed in this vast
    cave of monotony.

The physical pain will vanish soon,
 but the memory of those
 stark walls may well remain much longer.

August 1971

A NEW RELATIONSHIP

Since I have been in this bed
I have become rather intimate with my left knee-cap.
When the mood takes me, I get it out and stroke it,
or count the hairs on it, or even talk to it.
My left knee-cap and myself have struck up an
understanding, like man-to-man, that we shall
look after each other, and I have promised that
when we get out of here, I shall take it for a walk.

August 1971

THE WARD AT NIGHT

The lights are down very low.

There is very little movement, apart from a few vibrating nostrils, and a pair of white feet that occasionally wave to me from the opposite side of the room.

The old boy in the bed next to me is over ninety.

He has ceased his nocturnal moanings, and is quiet for a moment.

As I lie here I watch a lone fly encircling a lightbulb, and listen without interest to the hum of the central heating system.

I envy the night nurse as he slumbers in his chair.

I wish I could bloody well get to sleep!!

August 1971

THE NURSE

She is always there, here, never gone.

Her spotless uniform is stiff and reassuring, concealing a tiny waist, and a heart like the moon.

Her voice, her hands, and her feet go softly about their business.

Her cool, gentle fingers are ever ready to sooth the fevered brow of the old man, who has neither the strength nor the will, and of the young man, who gains his strength from her, and who loves her during the worst moments.

But she belongs to all men, for she must always be there.

August 1971

MATTHEW

Matthew's coming up for six
He loves a joke, he's full of tricks
He loves play-wrestling on the floor
And calling on the folks next door
Barbecues, and bonfire night,
And whacking the tennis ball out of sight,
He loves to run a race and win,
He loves to have his friends come in,
The garden after school and play
On a warm and sunny summer's day,
He loves to dance, he loves to sing,
He loves a slide, he loves a swing,
He loves his dad and he loves his mum,
But most of all he loves his thumb.

March 1984

"WE WILL ROCK YOU"

The curtain came up
    and the band were strummin',
Costumes 'n colours
    were a sight to see,
They started singin' 'n the
    place was hummin',
The thrill of the music
    was flowin' through me,
"We will rock you"
    was outa sight,
"We will rock you"
    was a wonderful night.

Singing was stunnin'
    and the lines were witty,
Made me laugh
    then made me cry,
The girls were funny
    and the boys were pretty,

Number after number
    was rockin' by,
"We will rock you" was
    a glittering light,
"We will rock you" was
    a wonderful night.

He raised his hands
    as our feet were tappin',
He raised them high
    and we knew the sign,
Two thousand hands now
    were suddenly clappin',
Eagerly clappin to the very
    last line,
"We will rock you" was
    a sheer delight,
"We will rock you" was
    a wonderful night.

The theatre was rockin' now
    as everyone adored 'em,
A thousand voices
    singin' along,
We stood to cheer 'em,
    clap 'em and applaud 'em,

All the way home
    I was singin' their song,
Queen's music,
    such a delight,
"We will rock you" was
    a wonderful night.

July 2006

"I may as well tell you, here and now,
that if you are going about the place
thinking things pretty,
you will never make a modern poet.
Be poignant, man, be poignant!"

P.G. Wodehouse

DIAMOND GEEZER

I am so very happy, that
I keep sittin' down to write
Songs to say I love ya
Poems showin' my delight
An' when somebody asks me, "Why?"
I explain I want to please 'er
An' the reason I'm so happy?
'Cos I am ya diamond geezer!!

To show that I'm so happy, I've
Been kissin' everythin' in sight
I've kissed the cat, the mat, my hat
I've kissed the teapot, kissed the light
I've kissed the toaster, kissed your text
I've even kissed the freezer
An' the reason I'm so happy?
'Cos I am ya diamond geezer!!

I want to take ya everywhere
To have excitin' trips
Like a sunny day in Hastings
And buy ya fish 'n chips
Or Rome, or Paris, or the Pyramids
Or the Leanin' Tower of Pisa
An' the reason that I feel this way?
'Cos I am ya diamond geezer!!

An' when I look upon ya
You have such lovely bits
Lovely teeth an' lovely eyes
Lovely hair an' lovely toes
You're my livin' masterpiece
You are my Mona Lisa
An' I want to tell ya all of this
'Cos I am ya diamond geezer!!

You tell me I'm a generous man
I spread me love around
Treat me friends 'n loved ones
Spend a couple of pound
Perish the thought I'd ever be
A scrooge, like Ebeneezer
And the reason that I feel like this?
I am ya diamond geezer!!

You make me feel I'm drunk with love
Celebrating every day
Here's to you, an' all ya charms
Wonderful in every way
I'll sip me gin, or scotch, or beer
Maybe Bacardi breezer
Intoxicated by the thought
I am ya diamond geezer!!

I feel I could do anything
Carry ya shoppin' from Timbuktu
Secure peace in the Middle East,
Deliver sunshine just for you
You make me feel so powerful
Like Buonaparte or Caesar
And the reason that I feel so strong?
I am ya diamond geezer!!

March 2010

A DAY IN THE BAY

We came today
To Robin Hood's Bay
Not to stay
Just for the day
Not in March, nor May
But on Boxing Day
To take a stroll
From Boggle Hole
A half-hour hop
Along the top
We walked in twos
With wonderful views
Of the sea and the sands
Whilst holding hands.

Steps leading down
Take us into the town
To gaze out on the bay
At the waves and the spray
Rolling their way
Onto rocks shiny grey

They'll be under the sea
When the day is done
When the tide has run
And night has begun.

But while it's away
On the sand we can play
With bat and ball
While the white gulls call
On a pebble-free patch
We play out our match
Till it's time to move on
Or the sands will be gone.

Pretty shells to be found
Fossils in the ground
Where the cliff has slipped down
In a soft, sticky brown
Onto the stones
Snapped by my phone's camera
For their myriad hues
Greys, browns and blues.

And so to Boggle Hole again
To cross the beck below the lane
Waters flowing off the land
Into the sea across the sand

Among the rock pools
Through the shingle
Seaweed, salt, fresh water mingle
Jurassic rock, wet stepping stones bare
Negotiated with the utmost care.

Then up the hill
Beside the ghyll
At the setting sun
Our day is run
We've had our fun
Our visit done
A day in the Bay
Second to none!

Boxing Day 2017

BOUND FOR AVIEMORE (via Stirling)

The Scottish landscape white with snow
Satnav tells the way to go
Across this land of scotch and curling
To the handsome fortress town of Stirling.

Leaving Kelso early morn
Light snow falling since the dawn
Four wheel drive and wipers whirling
My sights set on historic Stirling.

Nature's beauty surely means
I stop to photograph the scenes
As one by one they come unfurling
On my winter way to Stirling.

An open field, pure white and clear
I'm witnessing three running deer
Such privilege, my brain is churning
The bitter cold, my cheeks are burning.

To see the deer is truly thrilling
I feel like I have made a killing
To capture this exquisite sight
But this time they're in black and white.

Each time I stop I leave the car
Brave the cold, walk over the scar
Of the vehicle tracks, brown on the road
Car doesn't know that it's just snowed.

To click away and take my pics
Of winter wonderland in the sticks
Farmland, woodland, moorland, streams
Scenery the stuff of dreams.

I next pull off to snap the logs
Meet a logger walking his dogs
He works at Kielder further south
Steaming breath flows from his mouth.

His woolly hat spells out 'John Deere'
He's asking me 'What brings you here?'
I say I'm bound for Aviemore
There to find my sister's door.

It's been two years since last we met
I'll stay at hers, I'm in her debt
It's been too long, anyhow
So I can't wait to get there now!

Motorway's here, a faster ride
Pass Edinburgh on the starboard side
Good progress now, the car is willing
Scotland in the snow is thrilling.

The sun breaks through, further thrills
It's shining on the snow-white hills
Driving through this stunning light
As the 'Stirling' sign comes into sight.

And so I cruise into the town
Shrouded in its winter gown
Hotel Colessio to locate
'Excellent, it's not too late.'

Time for me to go explore
Stepping out the hotel door
In happiness, no trace of sorrow
I'll be in Aviemore tomorrow.

Colessio's lovely to a fault
Courtesy of grit and salt
Arrived here safely in the light
I shall sleep so well tonight!!!

29th December 2017

Paul and Dierdre and Carol and me.

Paul and Dierdre and Carol and me
Have met for the first time today
Not Paul, nor Carol, nor me actually
But Dierdre and me, any way.

We meet and greet and have a hug
Eyes are smiling, we say 'Hello'
In the warm, on the red stripy rug
Keep our coats, we're going to go.

Into the town, it's time to eat
A Ruby Murray with loads of chat
Park the car and cross the street
Find a table, park your hat.

It's been two years for Paul and me
He's found himself a girl
And now the world's his oyster
'Cause he's unearthed a pearl.

Dierdre's engaging and full of fun
Her eye's sparkle with each smile
Paul is happy, more than ever
Stands out a country mile.

Chatting over a leisurely meal
Of warming rice and curry
We raise a glass, we take our time
We're really in no hurry.

We talk of family, get up-to-date
Drive back home, we drink some tea
Leave them in peace, it's getting late
Paul and Dierdre, Carol and me.

Dec. 2017

DUNCAN, GRAEME, SAM – TWEED

From Aviemore on icy roads
Driving down, and watch your speed
To Oban, down the bar to meet
Duncan, Graeme, Sam – Tweed.

Two years or more since last we met
To meet again feels good indeed
Hugs and handshakes, smiles, beers
Duncan, Graeme, Sam – Tweed

And so to the fiddle, box and drum
They know it by heart, no need to read
Driving rhythms compel us to dance
Duncan, Graeme, Sam – Tweed.

Dancing feet and bodies swirling
Fantastic band, we're all agreed
Dancing warms, but smiles are warmer
Duncan, Graeme, Sam – Tweed.

Clapping, dancing, life-enhancing
Music to fulfil a need
Ceilidh music at its finest
Duncan, Graeme, Sam – Tweed.

1ˢᵗ Jan 2018

SKYLARK

For Wordsworth the skylark's
    an ethereal minstrel,
A pilgrim of the sky.
For Shelley it's a blithe spirit,
    showering the earth with melody,
Music from on high.

The skylark habitually sings while ascending,
Whilst hovering, winging, it's song unbroken
Sustained warbling, never ending,
Still singing sweetly whilst descending.

On a spring day on the downs down south,
Or on the northern moors
Sweet notes spring from each skylark's throat
Their symphony down from heaven pours.

From early February to June late,
They puff their plumage, thrust their breast
Defending territory or attracting a mate
To their open-country nest.

During the breeding season
They gather into flocks to feed
Their song increasingly silent
Contemplating the deed.

And when the skylarking is done
She will sit proudly on the nest
Then he again takes to the skies
Doing what he does best!

January 2018

"Poetry is the only art
people haven't yet
learnt to consume
like soup."

W.H. Auden

STICK WITH ME, HONEY

I have something to say
And it won't go away
So I ask you today
To stick with me.

I know I can reach you
I know I can teach you
I do beseech you
To stick with me.

Any kind of stick you choose,
Any kind of stick you use,
Stick of furniture
Walking stick
Stick of dynamite
Hockey stick
Stick of rock
Gear stick
Joystick
French stick
Stick for a drum
Stick out like a sore thumb

I may be a dry old stick
But I wish to twist, not stick.

For I do adore you
I'll try not to bore you
I do implore you
To stick with me.

I'll do my best
Not to be a pest
I do request
You stick with me.

Something special
May be emerging
So I am urging you
To stick with me.

I really do feel
I'm not a bad deal
I do appeal to you
To stick with me.

I'm quite polite
And I don't bite
I do invite you
To stick with me.

I'll never rest
Till I've passed your test
I do suggest
You stick with me.

I'm so afraid
All this will fade
Can I persuade you
To stick with me.

February 2018

THE PIG 'N PASTRY

The Pig 'n Pastry's on Bishy Road,
With Illy coffee, loose dress code,
Tasty Affogato shakes,
Courgette 'n pistachio cakes,
Exciting vibe, never gloomy,
Offering the Shroomalloumi.

Order avocado toast, from Steve,
Your warm and friendly host,
Or Julia, she runs the show,
Eating in, or good to go,
Best caff around by a country mile,
Always service with a smile.

The staff who serve do so with charm,
Efficiency, cool 'n calm,
Hot chocolate, pot of Rosie Lee,
Lemonade you, coffee me,
Delicious eating, you'll be smitten
Kitchen staff could cook for Britain.

Breakfast, lunches, afternoon tea,
Bacon butties, egg funghi,
Sharing tables, wifi free,
Brilliant conversationally,
A.m. queueing at the door
You'll be coming back for more!

February 2018

RHYMING ANTONYMS

Black white
   Wrong right
      In out
         All nowt
            Good bad
               Happy sad
                  This that
                     Uneven
 flat.
High low
  Yes no
     Come go
        Stop flow
           Suck blow
              Friend foe
                 Dull bright
                    Day
 night.
Slack tight
  Depth height
     Over under
        Whisper thunder

                        Foul fair
                            Here there
                                Slow quick
                                    Well sick.

Slow fast
   Future past
        Fore aft
            Sensible daft
                Forward reverse
                    Better worse
                        Hot cold
                            Nervy bold.
Accept reject
   Disdain respect
        Will won't
        Do don't
            Push pull
                Empty full
                    Awake asleep
                        Expensive cheap.
Laid-back pedantic
   Realistic romantic
        Large small

Short tall
    Skinny fat
        Bumpy flat
            Straighten bend
                Beginning end.

March 2018

IF SHAKESPEARE WAS SONNET, CAN I HAVE SOME, PLEASE!!

Shall I compare thee to a summer stay
At Hastings, Skegness, Whitley Bay?
Driving rain and rough winds
Do shake the darling buds of May.

Thou art more lovely than a trip to the sea
At Swanage, Southwold, Rhyl, Torquay
Seashells on beaches oh so long
As men can breathe or eyes can see.

And summer's lease hath all too short a date
With Brighton, Tenby or Margate
Glistening waters, golden sands
Compared to this thou art more temperate.

Sometime too hot, the eye of heaven shines
Upon you as a new-found love reclines
With Shakespeare's help I'm trying to say ...
To understand, please read between the lines!
March 2018

On a spanish strand.

Jeans rolled up, my feet are bare,
I'm feasting on the fresh sea air,
The water's cold, it makes me swear
As I step in the sea.

Walking on a spanish strand,
Precious sea-shells in my hand,
My toes into the shifting sand
Sink down deliciously.

The eager waves are low and white,
Above them sea-birds low in flight,
Bejewelled water, sunlight bright,
A walk, a wade, all free.

Grains of sand between my toes,
Across my feet as if it knows,
Caressing me with ebbs and flows
Gently goes the sea.

Relentlessly the white waves roll
Onto the land, into my soul,
Lifting me up, make me feel whole,
Just where I want to be!!

    March, 2018

MARATHON GIRLS

(For Julia and friends from the Pig 'n Pastry)

From Blackheath to
St James' Park
May your running
Be up to the mark.

Among the pack
Enjoy the craic
The playing bands
The waving hands.

Greenwich Park
The Cutty Sark
You're gonna deliver
As you cross the river.

Through the East End
Flat at least end
Going well still
At Tower Hill

Embankment, then
On to Big Ben
Parliament Square
Nearly there.

May you run tall
May your blisters be small
May you not hit the wall
So proud of you all!!

April 2018

LINK IN MY CHAIN

Please take note
Consider my quote
Wear my coat
Sail my boat
Cross my moat
Milk my goat
Watch my float
Get my vote
Ride in my car
Follow my star
Join my hike
Jump on my bike
Run in my lane
Ride on my train
Come down my line
And you'll be fine
Lighten your load
Walk down my road
You'll be on the up
Drinking from my cup
Gladden your heart

Climb onto my cart
Skip down my lane
Be a link in my chain
Don't follow the pack
Stroll down my track
Feel safe on my back
Feel warm in my sack
Why not take your feet
For a walk up my street
Take it slow down my byway
Get up speed on my highway
With plenty of leeway
Cruise on my freeway
Would love having you
Along my avenue
Lined with trees
Would be a breeze
You just can't fail
Along my trail
Learn to relax
Between my tracks
Your toes uncurled
Within my world
So give it a shot
And sail your yacht
Across my bay
Do not delay!

April 2018

CUP FINAL DAY

End of season
Cup Final Day
Thousands thronging
Wembley way.

Off the coach
In brand new suits
Brand new kit
Old favourite boots.

Walk out on
The hallowed turf
No finer football pitch
On Earth.

Final team talk
From the boss
Which way if we
Win the toss?

Play with the sunshine
At our backs
Sun in their eyes
In our attacks.

Their winger's nippy
Bit of flair
Be sure to let him
Know you're there.

Check your laces
Pads and socks
No mistakes
Inside the box.

Ref and captains
Shaking hands
In front of a
Hundred thousand fans.

Your Norman Hunters
Your Bobby Moores
Put your foot in
Early doors.

Your Ron Flowers
Your twin towers
Your Denis Law
Your Wembley roar.

Straight from kick-off
Push them deeper
Get a shot in
Test their keeper.

Pass and move
Play it quick
Hardly let them
Have a kick.

Your Jackie Milburns
Your Tony Books
Your Charlie Georges
Your Charlie Cooks.

Stay with the runner
Tracking back
Sliding tackle
Give him a whack!

Close them down
Nice and tight
They'll never score
If we play all night.

Their left back's slow
Bit of a kicker
Take him on
Fresh milk turns quicker.

Then our winger's away
He's in full flight
Past the full-back
Down the right

The cross comes over
Beautifully met
By our centre-forward
Into the net.

Head or knee
Foot or shin
We don't care
The balls gone in!

The bench are leaping
In the air
Shouting, screaming
Everywhere.

Come on ref
The time is up
Final whistle
We've won the cup.

Winning team
Walking proud
Show the trophy
To the crowd.

Losers look on
Battered, bruised
Losers' ribbons
Never used!!!

April 2018

RAVE ON AT THE CLARENDON

Leaving York for London town,
A1 busy drivin' down,
Find the Clarendon, Blackheath,
Room first floor, restaurant beneath,
Freshen up, come down, feelin' fine,
Front line table, French white wine,
Restaurant busy, a hundred guests,
Make clear their culinary requests.

Waitresses attentive, want to please,
Work the room with graceful ease,
My candle lit, 'twill melt the wax,
Another drink helps to relax,
Dinner served, tastin' good,
Room is buzzin' like it should.

Buddy Holly tribute man,
Warmin' up the best he can,
Checkin' lights 'n sound alike,
Testin' volume on the mike,

Adam Barnard is his name,
Singin' Buddy is his game,
Sing along if you can,
'Brown-eyed handsome man'.

'That'll be the day 'of 'True love ways',
In those later fifties days,
Couples now takin' to the floor,
'I guess it doesn't matter anymore',
'Listen to me' 'Not fade away',
'Rave on' at the Clarendon,
Friday night with 'Peggy Sue',
Adam, thanks to you!!

May 2018

SOMETHING GREAT!!!

This is Chate
A real good mate
Tall and strong
Stands up straight
Great big smile
Wide as a mile
Full of good cheer
Likes a beer.

        Clear the decks
        Here comes Bex
        Lovely lady
        Of the opposite sex
        She's Chate's wife
        Trouble 'n strife
        Together they're
        A wonderful pair.

She's a mum
He's a dad
Three beautiful
Young boys they've had
Johar, Rohan
And baby Hari
More Indian sounding
Than Patrick or Barry.

        Laughing, playing
        Growing strong
        Good natured children
        All day long.
        Johar likes to have a cuddle
        Rohan's walking through a puddle
        Hari leaves things in a muddle
        Accompanied by noise,

Hari mixes smiles with cries
Rohan with his big, brown eyes
Johar's into cake or fries
Three lovely little boys.

        Their Grandma's here
        Her name's Anita
        Grandma's never
        Come so sweeter
        The children though

    Know her as Nani (Narnie)
    She's good for chicken kebab
    Or a sarnie
    Fried potato cubes
    Samosa
    Courtesy of
    The Indian grocer

She'll cook for you
'Cos food is love
Her love, as warm
As a winter glove.

    Other grandparents
    Are Frances and Paul
    Come down from Durham
    To answer the call
    For babysitting anytime
    As babysitters they're sublime.

Lovely couple
Chate 'n Bex
Both top notch
In all respects
With their family
Bex 'n Chate
Really do have something Great!!!

May 2020

IMAGINATIVE PLAY

How would it be
To play some games
With famous names
Like Jesse James,
Judy Dench, Chris Hoy,
Vera Lynn, A.P. McCoy,
Well-known sirs and dames?

Play soccer
With a punk rocker
Or Liverpool docker.

Play cricket with Wilson Pickett.

Maybe lawn bowls
With Richard Coles,
Paul Scholes,
Or the Master of the Rolls.

Connect 4 with Patrick Moore
Jenga with Arsene Wenger.

Go ten pin bowling
With J.K. Rowling.

Play Monopoly
With Reece Topley.

A game of Scrabble
With Margaret Drabble.

How about rummy
With your mummy,
Or Twister
With your sister.

Try playing Polo
With Han Solo
Or a game of Solo
With Marco Polo.

Play saucy games
With E.L. James.

Or a spot of Trivial Pursuit
On the beach
With King Canute.

Table tennis
With Dennis the Menace,

Ping pong in Hong Kong
with Evonne
Goolagong.

Postman's knock
With Sandra Locke,
Captain Spock,
Quinton de Kock.

There's blind-man's-buff
With Brian Clough
Or hide and seek
With Tim Peake
Or Ruben Loftus-Cheek.

Charades with the Coldstream Guards.

Then musical chairs
With Pam Ayres,
Or Goldilocks and the three bears,
Downstairs.

How about some tiddlywinks
With Leon Spinks
Or the Rolling Stones
Or the Kinks.
Why not, me thinks

Challenge Minnie the Minx
To some golf on the links?

And who, I hear you cry,
Is for I-spy
With my little eye?
Why, it's Stephen Fry.

Let's play some chess
With Elliott Ness,
Or Good Queen Bess.

Let's hunt-the-thimble
With David Trimble.

Fly a kite down the lane
With Michael Caine,
Calamity Jane, David Blaine,
Or John Wayne.

Have a game of darts
With the Queen of Hearts.
You'll beat her at snooker
if she's got a verruca!

Pass the parcel to Barbara Castle.

Play Ludo with Brian May,
Cluedo with Cassius Clay.

Croquet with the Vicar of Bray,
With mallets and hoops
And Marjorie Proops.

Hugo Boss
Liked a game of Lacrosse,
Along with Joe Loss,
And Kate Moss.

Whether rugby or curling,
Shinty or hurling,
Whatever your name,
From wherever you came,
Or who's in the frame,
It's always the same,
It's only a game!!

Sept 2022

WORLD CUP 2022

World Cup in Qatar
Twenty twenty two
Never been held here before
Venues are brand new.

First time in the Middle East
So what about the stadia
Air conditioned, and overhead cover
To make the stadia shadier.

Fans arrive from far and near
Their favourite teams to see
But won't be drinking any beer
For most it's alcohol-free.

If temperatures are high
Then so's anticipation
They've come with flags 'n banners
Prepared for celebration.

Dressed in their team's colours
They've come to cheer them on

Willing them to victory
When the final whistle's gone.

Many in national costume
A multi-coloured scene
Of blue and yellow, red and white,
Orange, black and green.

Thirty two teams gathered
From nations far and wide
To represent their country
And play for national pride.

All teams have to qualify
For the finals in Qatar
So well done to everyone
For making it this far.

The tournament starts with groups of four
Each in with a shout
Without success you won't progress
And you will be knocked out.

You may be Spanish, Polish, Danish,
Belgian, Portuguese,
Possibly Argentinian, Korean,
Swiss or Senegalese,

Canadian, Costa Rican, Serbian,
Or Mexican,
All part of the Football World Cup lexicon.

Sixteen teams will make it through
Then eight, then four, then just the two
Disappointment for the many
Final glory for the few.

After all the running
Skill in passing and control
After all the tackles
Crosses, shots on goal
That went just wide
Or over the bar
All the checks by VAR
All the stout defending
All the clever tricks
Throw-ins, corners, offsides,
Penalties, free kicks
After all the headers
And fine goalkeeper saves
The chanting and the drumming
And Mexican waves
After all the brilliant goals
After all the fun
December eighteenth, twenty two
The trophy will be won.

One end of the stadium
Will ring with joyous cheers
The other will be heartbroken
And fighting back the tears.

But whether you're World Cup champions
Or just a local team
You're all winners in the end
As part of a wider theme.

For if you engage in football
Lowly or select
And treat each other face to face
With fair play and respect
Wherever you may come from
Whatever team you grace
If you can share a game that's fair
The world's a better place.

November 2022

SIMILIES : ANCIENT AND MODERN

As bold as brass
As green as grass
As funny as a farce
As raised as a glass.

    As black as night
    As high as a kite
    As fundamental
    As a human right.

As straight as an arrow
As pulled as a harrow
As pushed as a barrow
As marched from as Jarrow.

    As busy as a bee
    As jumpy as a flea
    As locking as a key
    As salty as the sea.

As hard-wearing as leather
As light as a feather
As purple as heather
As changeable as the weather.

    As thin as a rake
    As sweet as a cake
    As wriggly as a snake
    As phoney as a fake.

As dark as a cave
As silent as the grave
As surfed as a wave
As close as a shave.

    As old as the hills
    As grinding as mills
    As legal as wills
    As inky as quills.

As hard as nails
As windy as gales
As wind-blown as sails
As constraining as jails.

As cold as ice
As rolled as dice
As squeaky as mice
As egg-fried as rice.

As spoilt as a brat
As graceful as a cat
As blind as a bat
As unwelcome as VAT.

As smooth as satin
As Roman as Latin
As prescribed as statins
As early as matins.

As mad as a March hare
As grizzly as a bear
As challenging as a dare
As sat-in as a chair.

As close as a hug
As snug as a bug
As towing as a tug
As indifferent as a shrug.

As sly as a fox
As strong as an ox
As containing as a box
As tasty as a box of chocs.

       As white as a ghost
       As deaf as a post
       As warm as toast
       As warming as a Sunday roast.

As bright as a button
As greedy as a glutton
As sharp as a razor
As pinpoint as a laser.

       As bald as a coot
       As amphibious as a newt
       As hobnailed as a boot
       As pinstriped as a suit.

As gentle as a lamb
As tight as a clam
As holding as a dam
As sticky as jam.

As heavy as lead
As quiet as the dead
As toasted as bread
As king-sized as a bed.

As stubborn as a stain
As tiny as a grain
As unwelcome as pain
As damp as a drain.

As thick as thieves
As autumnal as leaves
As serving as Jeeves
As prolific as Greaves.

As heavy as tons
As loaded as guns
As clever as puns
As devoted as nuns.

As right as rain
As vast as a plain
As linked as a chain
As complex as a brain.

1st January 2023

ANXIETY

Been locked within a battle
Seemed sometimes like a war
I look back on my struggle
And all the pain I bore
The tide's been running over me
Stranded on the shore
Slowly, slowly drowning's
The analogy I draw.

I've tried my best to conquer it
I've fought it tooth and claw
It's hard to get your hat and coat
And stumble out the door
When every little daily task
Seems like a massive chore
Like a lion limping, with
A huge thorn in his paw.

I've often had not much to say
I must have been a bore
This condition angers me
Sticks there in my craw

Every forward step I take
It cracks me on the jaw
Knocks me back; how can I win
Down there on the floor?

But lately, and I know not why,
I'm doing more and more
Planning and embracing
What life has in store
Back to sharing laughter
With those that I adore
Maybe one day soon you'll hear
This lion start to roar!!

19th January 2023

BE THANKFUL FOR THE MUSIC

Be thankful for the music,
For the songs we sing,
Be thankful for the brass,
The wind and the string,
Give thanks for all the tapping,
The blowing and the ringing,
Give thanks for the musical joy they're bringing,
Thanks for the harmonies,
Thanks for the tunes,
Lyrics and symphonies,
Thank you for the spoons,
Harmonica and squeezebox,
Tissue paper, comb,
Tubular bells, vibraphone,
Pianos in the home,
Kettle, snare and cymbal,
Beat the big base drum,
Catchy tunes to whistle,
Melodies to hum,

Trombone, cornet, trumpet,
Drummer beats the skin,
Viola, cello, banjo,
Ukelele, violin.

Thank you for the washboard,
Thank you for the claves,
Thank you for the quavers,
Sitting on the staves,
Thank you for the saxophone,
Cors-anglais and lute
Thank you for the xylophone,
French horn, harp and flute.

Where would we be without
The strumming of guitars?
Without live music in our pubs
Or jazz played in our bars?
What if no-one ever went out
Busking any more?
We'd lose a most important aspect
Of our lives, for sure.

January 2023

"There was a young man called McNamitter,
Was blessed with prodigious diameter,
It was not his size that gave girls a surprise,
But his rhythm, iambic pentameter."

Anonymous

APPROPRIATELY NAMED

Penny's from heaven.
Flora loves her plant life.
Hazel, Holly, Willow, Linden,
And Rowan can be found in
Woods, parks and gardens.
Hazel is nuts, and Holly needs careful handling.
Ivy is quite the social climber, whilst
Rosemary and Basil have great taste.
Primrose, Iris, Lily, Violet, Poppy and
Daisy are all very pretty, and
Rose always smells so nice.

Britney is in France,
Barry's in South Wales,
Beverley is in Yorkshire, and
Douglas is on the Isle of Man.

Florence and Sienna are Italian, and
Sydney has a famous opera house
Named after him.

Tyler works on the roof,
Nick works at the police station,
Dean works at the cathedral,
Don teaches at the university,
Dan teaches judo, and
Belle is a campanologist.

Cerise, Scarlett and Ruby are
All redheads, and Bette, Betty
And Betsy all enjoy a flutter
At the races.

Jack is handy when a tyre needs changing.
Wayne is on the way down,
Peter is slowly grinding to a halt,
Jim's the one for a workout, and
Max does everything to the limit.

Shaun is a skinhead,
Andy can look after himself,
Ken knows what's what,
But can't say the same for Wally!

Christian believes in Jesus,
Grace gives thanks at dinner time,
While Neil does a lot of praying.

Ray always shines a light on things,
Crystal makes it all very clear, and
Sonny will brighten up your day.

Rory tends to sound like a lion.

Barney loves an argument,
Ernest can be rather serious,
Teddy is popular with children,
Buddy wants to be your friend, and
Philip is your man if you need a lift.

Cher likes to give to others, but
Heidi prefers to squirrel things away.

Harper and Mona are forever complaining, and
Vic gets up your nose.

June always comes round once a year, and
Carol turns up every Christmas time.

Eileen says she has trouble
Standing up straight,
Bob is up and down, and
Wanda easily strays off course.

Imogen is into photography,
Drew used to do artwork,

Reg is into car number plates,
And Mike has open nights at the pub.
Hew likes to wield an axe,
Lance prefers jousting, but
Rod is more into fishing.
Frank will give you the truth,
But Chantelle is sworn to secrecy.

Miles will go a long way,
Norman goes back a long way, and
Roman goes back even further.

Grant can get you some money,
Bill helps you to spend it each month, and
Will organises what's left when you are gone.

January 2023

I HAVE A NEW PAL

I have a new pal,
His name is Ashley,
He's known as Ash,
He calls me Al.

Ash is courteous, respectful, polite,
I am spontaneous, fly like a kite.

Cuttin' a dash,
Al 'n Ash,
Out on the lash,
Ash 'n Al.
Needin' more rationale.

Cheeky boys,
But not too brash,
I like Pavarotti,
He likes The Clash, and Bowie,
For me, Johnny Cash.

Al and Ash
Less fashion, more passion
More cedar-clad
Less pebbledash.

Ash is a scaffold man,
Spends his days dreamin' of poles,
I am a football man,
Spend my days reliving goals.

Ash and I were footballers,
He played for Selby Town,
I played for Bexley, National League,
When refs were slow
And balls were brown.

I was a striker, goal scorer,
Ash was a centre back,
Had we ever opposed on the pitch
He would have given me a smack,
A crack, a whack.

But I took whacks aplenty,
Kept coming back for more,
I don't hurt him by kickin' back,
I hurt him when I score.

But Ash and I, we're buddies,
We have a common bond,
An inherent love of banter,
His tongue is like a wand,
Orchestratin' conversation,
Always has a word to say,
If I can get in edgeways
I may have a say today.

Ashley 'n I,
Al 'n Ash,
Two icons,
Asterisk 'n Hash,
Perfect pairing
Like sausage 'n mash,
Like BMW or Frazer Nash.

Both clean-shaven,
No beard or moustache,
Two smooth players
Makin' a splash.

Ash is a DJ
Spinnin' the vinyl,
Presley Elvis
Or Ritchie Lionel,

Rotten Johnny
Or Tyler Bonnie,
White Barrie
Or Styles Harry.

While Ash is DJing in a club
I read poems in a pub,
About a geezer who kisses his freezer,
Or the blind-man's-buff
Of Black Dog stuff.

Ash 'n Al,
We like a beer
Up Yorkshire way,
We love it here.

Warm or freezin'
Whatever the weather,
Ash an' I
When we're together,
Face to face
Or side by side,
We're brother travellers
Both enjoyin' the ride.

March 2023

THE GARDEN ROOM

El Campello in the park,
Lovely café, just my mark,
Warm welcome, family run,
Spot-on service, sense of fun.

Child friendly, stuff to do,
Tasty menu, food is too,
Coffee, soft drinks, beer or fizz,
The Garden Room is just the bizz.

Hot lunches, if you're in the mood,
You're eating freshly home-made food,
Falafel wrap or soup of the day,
Don't wanna go, just wanna stay.

And stay some more for a cake and tea,
A detox smoothie is working for me,
Tostados, baps, croissants, wraps,
Milkshakes galore,
I'll be back for sure!!

April 2023

WONDERFUL AFTERNOON IN BUSOT

Busot twenty twenty three,
Great, great afternoon for me,
Sunday, in the top town square,
Something wonderful right there,
Where for International Day,
For only very little to pay,
They held inside a white marquee
An awesome music jamboree.

Flamenco, traditional Spanish fashion,
Danced with typical Spanish passion,
Staccato rhythms to the fore,
Staccato heel-stamp on the floor
Creating drama in the dance,
Entertainment to enhance,
Men and Women, dancers mixed,
Audience looking on transfixed.

Troupe of three now take the stage,
Boys and girls of any age
Sit and clap and sing along
To a repertoire of Spanish song,
Familiar songs the people love
Fit the occasion like a glove.

And so to the brilliant rock 'n roll band,
Which soon sees everybody stand
To move, and dance some rock or pop,
Dancing's great, don't want to stop,
Two guitars, lead, base, and drums,
Wishing the last song never comes,
Such smiles, and happiness and fun
Under the shimmering Busot sun.

30th April 2023

THE PASTA MENU
(Robyn's favourite)

Flour and eggs for pasta dough,
Just ask Alessandro,
Italian chef extraordinaire,
Makes all the pasta with love and care.

What shape shall we choose?
Which design?
Your preferred choice
Won't always be mine.

Long wiggle tubes of plain spaghetti
Are served with Bolognese sauce,
I prefer my Bolognese sauce
With fettuccini, of course.

And if it's ribbons you like to eat,
Maybe tagliolini would taste a treat,
For a blow-out you'll choose a large lasagne,
Can't beat it with plenty of garlic bread, can ya?

Good things come in small parcels
As with your ravioli,
Delicate flavours lie within,
So try to eat it slowly.
Pesto and penne pasta
Are great with parmigiano,
Popular in Italia
From Milano to Positano.

Other tube pastas are cannelloni
Calamarata and macaroni,
Vermicelli is thin round strands
When it's been through Alessandro's hands.

Other pasta with food inside
May well be tortellini,
Or tortelloni for a change,
Much preferred to a plate of blini.

Spatzie is shaped for fun,
More parcel-force with agnolotti,
But now our pasta race is run,
So finish with coffee and biscotti.

May 2023

GOLDEN OLDIES

'Begin the beguine' from Artie Shaw
   in nineteen fifty six
Travelling 'Route sixty six'
Is where the Stones get their kicks.
Pat Boone confesses 'That's my desire'
Julie Driscoll's 'Wheels on fire'
Springsteen sings 'This gun's for hire'
Feliciano's 'Light my fire'.
The Beach boys were having 'Fun, fun, fun'
George Harrison saying 'Here comes the sun'
Adam Ant cried 'Stand and deliver'
Christie sailed on the 'Yellow River'.
Don Estelle sang 'Whispering grass'
Blondie had a 'Heart of glass'
Don Partridge was a one-man-band
Bass drum, kazoo, guitar in hand
Sang about his woman Rosie
Dave Dee, Mick, Titch 'n Dozy
With the 'Legend of Xanadu'
And 'Zabadak', to name but two.
Status Quo 'Down deeper 'n down'

George Melly loved his 'Fanny Brown'
Leiber 'n Stoller's reputation grew
With songs like 'Hound Dog' 'n 'Loving You'.
Alan Clark 'n The Hollies 'Just one Look'
'Sylvia's Mother' from Dr Hook
James Brown's 'Momma has a brand new bag'
'Don't try this at home' warned Billy Bragg.
'Way down yonder in New Orleans'
Not Björk's voice, and not Al Green's
But in fifty nine by Freddie Cannon
Followed closely by Del Shannon
With hits like 'Runaway', 'Hats off to Larry'
'The Tide is high' for Debbie Harry
Thin Lizzie drank 'Whiskey in the jar'
So 'Baby you can drive my car'.
From the album 'Rubber Soul'
Beatles style rock 'n roll
John, George, Ringo, Paul
'Another suitcase in another hall'
Madonna starring in Evita
Sinitta's voice could not be sweeter
A deeper sound from Nina Simone
Soul funk from Sly and the Family Stone.
'The Wanderer' came from The Belmonts and Dion
'King of the rodeo' sang the Kings of Leon
Formed in Nashville, from the States
Mark Knopfler fronting Dire Straits
'Money for nothing', 'So far away'

Dylan suggesting 'Lay, Lady, Lay'
Otis Redding on the 'Dock of the bay'
Relaxing on Lou Reed's 'Perfect day'.
Norah Jones pleads 'Come away with me'
The Beatles suggesting 'Let it be'
For Herman's Hermits 'There's a kind of hush'
'The Power of love' from Jennifer Rush.
'Wonderwall' sang the Gallagher boys
'Hang on Sloopy' advised the McCoys
'Stay with me' implored Sam Smith
Stephen Stills said 'Love the one you're with'.
The Faces got high in 'Itchycoo Park'
Springsteen's 'Dancing in the dark'
'Can't start a fire without a spark'
'Glad all over' felt Dave Clark.
Judy Garland sang in 'Wizard of Oz'
Harry Styles singing 'As it was'
First album included 'Sign of the times'
'How do I live?' asks LeAnn Rimes.
'Set fire to the rain' suggested Adele
Chris Rea travelled 'The road to hell'
'Good morning freedom' said Madeline Bell
Chuck Berry reckoned 'You never can tell'.
'Like toy soldiers' from Eminem
'Man on the moon' with R.E.M.
Van Morrison sang with his band, Them
'Oh little town of Bethlehem'
Very well-loved Christmas Carol

Vera Lynn sang 'Roll out the barrel'
To British troops in World War Two
'It's all over now, Baby Blue'.
A number penned and performed by Dylan
Mark Knopfler says 'let's stop the killin''
A serious message in 'Brothers in Arms'
Church choirs singin' hymns 'n psalms.
'The autumn leaves' from Nat King Cole
Jerry Lee Lewis sang rock 'n roll
Best of all the rock 'n roll choir
'Breathless' and 'Great balls of fire'
A rock 'n roll piano great
Ricky Nelson pointing out 'It's late'
'There's a sweet fraulein down in Berlin town'
In Travellin' man, while Joe Brown
Was showin' his 'Picture of You'
'Pinball Wizard' came from The Who
'Bohemian Rhapsody' from Queen
'Let's stay together' cried Al Green.
'Let's stick together' implored Bryan Ferry
'In the summertime' said Mungo Jerry
Val Doonican wanted to 'Walk tall'
For Abba, 'The winner takes it all'.
The Kinks sang about a girl called 'Lola'
Who got to drinkin' cherry cola.
Ed Sheeran sang of the 'Castle on the hill'
His song, 'Perfect', was top of the bill.
George Harrison said 'that's the way it goes'

Whilst Frank Sinatra 'took the blows'
In 'My Way', 'as the record shows'
Paul Young admits 'everybody knows'
'For he's the type of guy'
'Who gives a girl the eye'
'I love 'em and I leave 'em'
'Break their hearts 'n deceive 'em'.
Shane MacGowan and the Pogues
Were founded in King's Cross
Pogue Mahone means 'Kiss my arse'
They couldn't give a toss.
'Fairytale of New York'
Best ever Christmas Song for some
Dexy's midnights, U.B.40
Bands from Birmingham.
'Fields of gold' from the pen of Sting
Chuck Berry holding his 'Ding-a-ling'
Bagpipes playing the highland fling,
For 'Brown girl in the ring'.
The lovely Taylor, Alison Swift
Born in Pennsylvania
With millions of adoring fans
Echoing Beatlemania
The Beatles sang please 'Love me, do'
Followed by 'From me to you'
'Michelle', 'I want to hold your hand'
From the brilliant Liverpool-based band.
Billy Ray Cyrus has a daughter, Miley

She must make him full of pride
Massive following worldwide
Superstar, just like Kylie.
Billy Ray had an 'Achy, breaky heart'
Mark Knopfler, 'Though we're far apart
Wear your ruby shoes when you're far away
So home in your heart you'll always stay.'
Dolly Parton and Kenny Rogers
Were country music's dream team
Jolene, Ruby and Lucille are
Lonely 'Islands in the stream'.
Bruno Mars and the Hooligans
With 'Billionaire' and 'Nothing on you'
Singles 'Haven't found you yet'
And 'Dance with me', from Blue.
Tom, George, Roy, Bob 'n Jeff
Sadly only two guys left
The Travelling Wilburys was their name
Good friends jamming was their game.
Petty, Harrison, Orbison, Lynne
Dylan, set out with nothing planned
'Handle with care' will always be there
For this fantastic band.
In the fifties Doris Day
'Through the grapevine', Marvyn Gaye
Roy Wood down 'Blackberry Way'
'This year's love' from David Gray.
'Love is all around' sang Marti Pellow

'Good year for the roses' and Elvis Costello
'Angel' in Robbie Williams' tones
'Honky tonk women' from the Rolling Stones.
'I can see clearly now' Johnny Nash
'Walk the line' with Johnny Cash
Don McLean's 'American Pie'
'Them old boys drinking whiskey 'n rye'.
Elvis Presley's 'Stuck on you'
Orbison's missing 'California blue'.
On vinyl, cd, Spotify
They'll make you smile, they'll make you cry
They'll make you dance, they'll make you fly
For Golden Oldies will never die!!

June 2023

PARTY INVITATION

Arrive at mine with a happy heart,
Arrive by limo or horse 'n cart,
Arrive by cab, or car, or bus,
But arrive you must.

For you can be wined,
You can be dined,
In company refined,
Away from the daily grind,
If you've a mind,
Wipe your feet on the mat,
Take off your hat
Come in for a chat.
Ideal location,
Outstanding conversation,
No hesitation,
Have a libation,
Tea, coffee, coke or booze
There for you to choose.

Dance by the jukebox,
If you're feeling fit,
The all-year-round house
Should you wish to sit.
Don't miss the best gig in York,
And bring your own
Knife and fork.

June 2023

CULHAM REUNION 2023

Keith Cuzz, headteacher extraordinaire
Teaching with West country flair
Spare time D.J. loves Argyle
His team, this year, have made him smile.

John Beasley, over from Vannes in France
A select gathering to enhance
Main French, not keen on swimmin'
World expert at pullin' women.

Up from the Land of our Fathers
Michael's here from Abergavenny
He'll have a drink or three tonight
And maybe one too many.

Recently Bruce Springsteen
Played at Villa Park
Mike's hoping this year Villa
Won't be dancing in the dark.

Peter Smith from West Sussex way
Formerly of Minnis Bay
Captained our college football team
International Head of some esteem.

George Weech's with us on this day
His winning smile shining bright
Retired now but he remains
Youth Service supremo on the Isle of Wight.

Dave Griffiths, known as Dave the Match
P.E. teacher, special needs
Favourite colour, pale blue
Expert in Man. City deeds.

Geoff Granville, cheerful all the way,
His smile would brighten up your day
Played for college between the sticks
With reliable hands and booming kicks.

Sadly Chris Hill can't be here
He's taken in people from Ukraine
Providing them with a temporary home
A generous act to ease their pain.

Peter Raper hails from Thorne
All-round sporting chap of note
Always loved a game to play
Now lives 'n plays in the U.S.A.

Chris Gee's up from Stoneleigh, Surrey
Laid back, never known to hurry
Out on the downs on Derby day
To wager his few bob each way.

I'm Alan Horne, I used to spend
My college mornings in my bed
Today, often up with the dawn
And write my poetry instead.

Late sixties when we all first met
Fifty plus years, still going yet
May all our days be sweet
Until next time we meet!!

1st July 2023

JUST MY CUPPA

Friday mornin' goin' down
Found myself in Yeadon town
North of Bradford, north of Leeds
Offering what a visitor needs
Fuel, parkin', shoppin' galore
Charity, Wetherspoon, hardware store
Morrisons for all things to eat
But 'Just My Cuppa' for a special treat.

This café sure has what it takes
Toasted stuff, Friday cakes
Bloomin' good things for brunch
Bowls of goodness for your lunch
They'll adapt to your needs of diet
No music blaring, blessed quiet
Fairtrade coffee, Italian style
Best caff in town by a country mile.

The vibe is great, the staff are fun
For quality this is the one!!

14th July 2023

ORKNEY TRIP

From Aviemore, through Inverness
We take the route to Wick,
It's half past four o'clock a.m.,
The road is clear and quick.

At John O'Groats the road bears left,
In view is Dunnet Head,
British mainland's northern tip,
We need the port instead.

We're on the Orkney ferry
Departing from Gill's Bay,
Across the breezy Pentland Firth
Onto Ronaldsay.

Past Stroma, uninhabited
We're clear of Inner Sound,
Heading into Scapa Flow
Where the Royal Oak went down.

Docking at St Margaret's Hope,
Churchill's Barriers to cross,
Built at once at his command
At the navy's major loss.

Road takes us on to Skara Brae
Seaside village from Stone Age times
Houses, furnitures made from stone
Designed for northern climes.

Second ferry from Houton Bay
For a short trip onto Hoy
Me, Carol, Colin, Angus, Hannah
And their little baby boy.

A charming bungalow awaits
By the waters of Mill Bay
Where oystercatchers grace the shore
And purple heathers lay.

Colonial style conservatory
With decking all around,
Steps down to the shoreline
Where arctic terns abound.

With blood-red bill and coal-black head,
They feast on shellfish in the sand,

And glide upon the bracing air
Of this wild, Viking land.

Primroses and daffodils,
Swathes of bluebells in the spring,
Orchids and wild irises,
Hen harrier on the wing.

Find the secret garden,
A sheltered, magic haven,
To sit and watch the Orkney sky
Of osprey, gull and raven.

Find the stony, trickling burn
Flowing by the former mill,
Formed a million years ago,
The water flowing still.

Up to the wartime cemetery,
Rows of white gravestones,
Young men cut down in their prime,
Never to make old bones.

Park the car by Rackwick beach,
Climb the hill to St John's Head,
Gaze down upon Old Man of Hoy,
Famous stack of sandstone red.

Teatime snacks in Beneth'ill caff,
Mainland Orkney in full view,
Sharing stories over tea,
Old friendships with the new.

Back at the ranch the fire's lit,
The wine is nicely chilled,
Prosecco bubbles soon are poured,
Our glasses duly filled.

Evening meal is on the go,
Chris de Berg sings us along
Maybe Kris Kirstofferson,
Or a Willie Nelson song.

Next day our breakfast time is slow,
Eggs and toast are on the go,
Chewing the fat, dog on the mat,
Outside the storm winds blow.

The wild wind continues to blow,
As into the calm museum we go,
To learn of World Wars One and Two,
And the ships of Scapa Flow.

Thence to Longhope Village,
To the Island's only store,

And the Island's only petrol pump,
Where the lifeboat comes ashore.

During supper a vivid rainbow
Spans above the bay,
An arch of multicolouredness,
Soon to fade away.

Early morning packing up,
Leaving around eight,
Ferry back to Mainland,
Sure must not be late.

At Kirkwall out across the bay,
Two giant cruise liners draw near,
American tourists scour the shops
For an Orkney souvenir.

We stop en route for a chapel
Beautiful, ceiling to floor,
Created and painted by two Italian
Prisoners of war.

Pentland Firth for the ferry back
Has a mercifully calm sea,
Farewell Orkney, thanks for now
From the others, the dog, and me.

August 2023

DO NOT TOUCH IT!!

Holy cow!
That's obscene,
Do not touch it,
Can't be clean,
Totally gross,
Know what I mean?
There's no knowing
Where it's been.
Mouldy, turning
Vivid green,
Glowing with
A shiny sheen,
Slimy droplets
In between
Most gruesome thing
I've ever seen!!

September 2023

FOR FRANCES AND PAUL

Have a great time on your Aegean cruise,
Sun hats and sun cream, the best things to use,
Good to wear sandals instead of your shoes,
Whilst taking in all those Greek island views,
The greens and the blues of varying hues,
Enjoy the food, moussaka and stews,
Enjoy the history, things to peruse,
Hope the excursions have modest queues,
Enjoy the churches, rest in the pews,
Have a stress-free trip, no tempers to lose,
Keep calm at all times, no blowing a fuse.
Go where you will, have what you choose
Relax with a puzzle or two, to amuse,
Maybe a crossword, work out some clues,
Don't be tempted by all the cheap booze,
And may your return bring only good news.

Sept 2023